We Go on a
School Bus

by Joanne Mattern

LOOK! BOOKS™

Red Chair Press   Egremont, Massachusetts

Look! Books are produced and published by Red Chair Press:

Red Chair Press LLC   PO Box 333   South Egremont, MA 01258-0333

www.redchairpress.com

 FREE Educator Guides at www.redchairpress.com/free-resources

Publisher's Cataloging-in-Publication Data

Names: Mattern, Joanne, 1963–
Title: We go on a school bus / by Joanne Mattern.
Other Titles: School bus

Description: Egremont, Massachusetts : Red Chair Press, [2019] | Series:
    Look! books. Ways we go | Includes glossary and "Good to Know" fact
    boxes. | Interest age level: 004-007. | Includes bibliographical
    references and index. | Summary: "What to expect from a trip on a
    school bus."--Provided by publisher.

Identifiers: ISBN 9781634406352 (library hardcover) | ISBN 9781634406475
    (paperback) | ISBN 9781634406413 (ebook) | LCCN 2018955669

Subjects: LCSH: Transportation--Juvenile literature. | School buses--
    Juvenile literature. | CYAC: Transportation. | School buses.

Classification: LCC HE152 .M384 2019 (print) | LCC HE152 (ebook) | DDC 388
    [E]--dc23

Photo credits: All iStock except for the following: pp. 7, 12 Shutterstock.

Printed in United States of America

0519 1P CGF19

Table of Contents

Going to School

It's time to go to school! Some children walk to school. Others get a ride from Mom or Dad. Many children take a bus to school. Let's find out more.

A Special Bus

A school bus looks different from a city bus. School buses are bright yellow. This makes them easy to see. A school bus might be small. Or it might be very big!

School buses are yellow with black because it's the easiest color to see in all types of weather.

At the Bus Stop

Children wait at the **bus stop**. Sometimes parents wait here too. It is important to stay out of the road. Watch for the bus to come.

The Bus is Here!

Here comes the bus! Yellow lights flash as the bus slows down. Then red lights flash when the bus stops. Little stop signs pop out from the side of the bus. All cars and trucks have to stop and wait.

Step Inside

The doors open. Now you can climb the steps up into the bus. Say hello to the driver!

Inside the Bus

Find a seat. School bus seats are tall and **padded**. Some buses have seat belts. A **bus monitor** helps students. The monitor makes sure everyone stays safe.

The bus monitor may be a teacher or parent. Always obey the monitor to stay safe.

The bus drives through the neighborhood. More children get on at each stop. There is lots of talking and laughing on the bus. It can be loud!

It is okay to have fun, but be sure to stay in your seat when the bus is moving!

Getting to School

The bus drives up to the school. It pulls up to the curb. The doors open. Everyone gets off. Be careful on the steps!

19

Going Home

The school bus will be back to take you home. Stand up when you see your stop. Say goodbye to the driver. Make sure all the cars are stopped so you can get home safely!

Good to Know

In 1939, a rule was made that all school buses in the USA would be the same yellow color.

Words to Know

bus monitor: a person on a school bus who helps the driver and keeps students safe

bus stop: a place where people wait for the bus

padded: covered with soft material

Learn More at the Library

Books (Check out these books to learn more.)

Garrett, Winston. *Let's Ride the School Bus!* PowerKids Press, 2015.

Jennings, Rosemary. *Safe on the School Bus.* PowerKids Press, 2017.

Murray, Julie. *School Buses.* Abdo Kids, 2016.

Index

About the Author

Joanne Mattern has written hundreds of nonfiction books for children. She likes writing about different people and places. Joanne lives in New York State with her family.